WWII

D-DAY AND THE PROVIDENCE OF GOD

Study Guide

VISION FORUM
Ministries®

First Printing

"Where there is no vision, the people perish."

The Vision Forum, Inc.
4719 Blanco Rd., San Antonio, Texas 78212
1-800-440-0022
www.visionforum.com

ISBN 978-1-937460-05-1

Cover Design by Austin Collins
Typography by Justin Turley

All Scripture references taken from the King James Version, unless otherwise noted.

Printed in the United States of America

Other Curriculum Sets from Vision Forum

Law & Government: An Introductory Study Course

The Young Ladies' Study Course for Proper Writing

Biblical Economics: A Complete Study Course by R.C. Sproul, Jr.

The History of Christianity and Western Civilization

The History of the World Collection

Into the Amazon: One Lost World, Thirty Men, Seven Mysteries

Table of Contents

WWII

D-DAY AND THE PROVIDENCE OF GOD

Study Guide

Episode 1

The Theological Significance of the Second World War

In Episode 1, we will examine how that the Second World War and D-Day itself occurred within a broader context than simply a great military conflict, as did the philosophies, alliances, rules of engagement, and military and political decisions that drove the war and its many battles. Adolf Hitler and his worldview, though taken to a horrific extreme, were ultimately an extension of key religious commitments which came to define the modern world in the 20th century. Winston Churchill represented very different commitments, those which emerged from an ancient order associated with the ethics of Christendom. The backdrop of Episode 1 will center in the city of Rome, whose legacy of empire influenced Hitler's vision of global conquest. We will explore Rome's significance as a strategic military objective during the war and why the Allies desired to retake Rome from Hitler. We will also look at the ethical implications of a great massacre committed by the Nazis in Rome before it fell to the Allies.

1. What is theology?

2. How do cultures reflect the theology of a people?

3. What does it mean for a nation to be a Christian nation?

4. What is Christendom?

5. How does the religious worldview of Winston Churchill contrast with Adolf Hitler's religious worldview?

6. What are some of the basic tenet's of Winston's Churchill's worldview?

7. Complete this statement by Winston Churchill regarding the Battle of Britain: "Upon this battle depends the survival of...."

8. How did ancient Rome influence Hitler's vision of the Third Reich?

9. What great icon of ancient Rome became a staging ground for Nazi marches?

10. What are some of the symbols of Rome which were embraced by the Third Reich?

11. What were three philosophical influences in Hitler's life?

12. What is the name of the controversial, nineteenth-century German composer who Hitler admired?

13. There has been much debate and discussion about the Vatican's silence regarding Nazi atrocities and the possible complicity of the Vatican with the Nazis during World War II. Of special concern has been the role of the Vatican during the Nazi occupation of Rome. What should the role of the true Church be in the face of tyranny, statism, and abject evil?

____

____

____

____

14. What is the name of massacre perpetrated by the Nazis in Rome in March of 1944? How many Italian civilians were murdered as part of this mass execution?

____

____

____

____

15. What event exposed Erich Priebke and led to his extradition from Argentina to Italy to be tried for his involvement with the massacre in Rome?

____

____

____

____

16. Should men who are alive today be held accountable for murders committed close to seven decades ago during the Second World War?

____

____

____

____

17. What was the outcome of Priebke's trial?

18. What leader recognized the significance of the Allies defeating Hitler's stronghold at Rome in terms of what the city represented as a symbol of empire?

19. The fall of Rome in 1944 was the culmination of what major Allied campaign?

20. What is the connection between the date that Rome was liberated from the Nazis and the invasion of Normandy?

Bible Memory Verses

"The wicked walk on every side, when the vilest men are exalted." (Psalm 12:8)

"For every tree is known by his own fruit. For of thorns men do not gather figs, nor of a bramble bush gather they grapes. A good man out of the good treasure of his heart bringeth forth that which is good; and an evil man out of the evil treasure of his heart bringeth forth that which is evil: for of the abundance of the heart his mouth speaketh. (Luke 6:44-45)

Episode 2
The Strategic Overview

In Episode 2, we will study the foolishness of appeasement within the context of the conquest of Europe by Hitler. Our strategic overview will compare the relationship of France and Germany over generations, with particular focus on the Treaty of Versailles that was signed at the close of the First World War, which laid the groundwork for Hitler's rise to power and desire to subjugate France. We will discuss France's overtures of appeasement and how this led to the country's fall to the Nazis and the rise of the Vichy government. We will also look at England's attempts at appeasement under the leadership of Prime Minister Neville Chamberlain, as well as the subsequent rise of Sir Winston Churchill, who clearly understood Hitler's real intentions as a tyrant and who spoke prophetically concerning the threat. We will seek to explain the providential meaning and relationship of the Allies' early defeats at Dieppe and Dunkirk and note how Churchill's resolve in launching the Battle of Britain helped check Hitler's great designs to conquer Great Britain. Ultimately we will see that bullies cannot be left to their own devices when liberty is at stake; they must be challenged with clear resolve.

1. In what way is the faith of the people of a nation linked to their national identity?

2. Why do nations become vulnerable to oppression when they lose their identity as a people?

3. In the 16th century Reformation, Christianity was dealt a horrific blow by the Roman Catholic Church when tens of thousands of Christian men, women and children known as French Huguenots were put to the sword as part of the St. Bartholomew's Day Massacre. What possible impact did the removal of Reformation Christianity have on the identity of the French people?

4. In what way has the relationship of France and Germany over the years been like that of feuding families?

5. What were the implications of the Treaty of Versailles for the people of Germany?

6. What was the path to subjection by the Nazis that France took from the conclusion of the first World War to their defeat and the occupation of France?

7. What were the likely motivations of Adolf Hitler in invading and subjugating France?

8. What French World I hero surrendered France to the Nazis, and what was the name of the new collaborationist government between France and the Nazis that he spearheaded?

9. What was one of the key, egregious demands that the Nazis made on the Vichy government in France?

10. How did the Nazis demonstrate their arbitrary and wicked behavior as masters over the French people?

11. Upon the establishment of Vichy government, who became the recognized leader of the Free French Forces who continued to resist Nazi subjugation?

12. While Hitler had been invading territories outside Germany throughout the 1930s, what event marks the beginning of World War II, according to most historians.

13. What Scripture passages might apply to the issue of dealing with bullies? What is the duty of Godly leaders in the face of wickedness? Defend your position from the Scriptures.

14. Who was the leading prophetic voice regarding Hitler's real intentions, and what notable phrase did he use to describe Hitler's advances in the 1930s?

15. What does the Bible say about the duty of Christians to endure and persevere in the face of trials? How did Winston Churchill model this as an international leader in the fight against Nazism?

16. In contrast to Winston Churchill, what British Prime Minister personified the doctrine of appeasement? What was the name of the accord he signed with Hitler that best represents this capitulation?

17. What was the "Miracle of Dunkirk"?

18. What key battle between England and Germany prevented Hitler from landing troops on the English shore and subjugating the British Isles?

19. Did the sovereign God decree and ultimately oversee all the events of the second World War—including the rise of Adolf Hitler, the subjugation of Europe under Nazi rule, and the many crimes which took place under the Third Reich?

20. How does a strong appreciation for providence give hope in the midst of trials?

Bible Memory Verses

"They that forsake the law praise the wicked: but such as keep the law contend with them." (Proverbs 28:4)

"If thou faint in the day of adversity, thy strength is small." (Proverbs 24:10)

Episode 3
The Theology of Leadership on D-Day

Episode 3 presents a fascinating study of a biblical perspective on leadership during the Second World War. We will examine the character and leadership skills of eight key decision-makers in the European theater of war—President Roosevelt, General Eisenhower, General Bradley, General Patton, Winston Churchill, General Montgomery, General Rommel, and Adolf Hitler. We will note the differences between bold confidence in a holy outcome and leading through courage and trust, and leadership styles which are dependent on fear and intimidation. And we will see how all of these issues were decisive in Normandy on June 6, 1944 as D-Day operations commenced. Each one of these leaders has clear lessons—both good and bad—that, if learned, will enable us to become more effective leaders with the challenges we face today.

1. How should a leader view the nature of authority regarding those above and below him in rank?

2. What character traits will best enable a leader to properly respond to orders from a superior?

3. How did General Eisenhower demonstrate the proverbial instruction that "in abundance of counselors, there is victory?" (Proverbs 11:14, NAS)

4. Why would this principle be particularly important for the Supreme Allied Commander?

5. For a military operation, what preparation questions need to be addressed by the leader?

6. What advantages might accrue from knowing about the personality, beliefs, victories and defeats in your adversary's past?

7. How did General Patton use that knowledge to his own advantage in North Africa?

8. How did his ability to delegate authority work to the advantage of President Franklin Roosevelt over his rival Adolph Hitler?

9. What differing multi-generational visions did the three political leaders project?

10. What are some ways that Adolph Hitler's presuppositions regarding genetics, race, and nationality affected his policies toward his own citizens and those he conquered?

11. How did General Eisenhower's sense of accountability affect his relationships with Generals Bradley and Patton? How did it affect his approach to the outcome of D-Day?

12. When a subordinate officer's strategic vision differs from his superior's, what should he do? What did General Montgomery do when he differed with Eisenhower?

13. How did Hitler's attempts to lead by fear and intimidation affect the outcome of D-Day?

14. What character traits did General Eisenhower admire in General Bradley?

15. Winston Churchill lived through the ebbing away of the principles of Christendom in his lifetime, but viewed the Nazi threat as the possible death-blow to that civilization. Was National Socialism a real threat to the continuance of the values of the historic Christian past?

16. The Bible has much to say regarding Christian perseverance. How did Winston Churchill evidence that virtue, and how did he communicate it to others?

17. How did FDR inspire hope and perseverance to the American people?

18. What are some examples of successful leadership styles on the actual beaches and paratrooper landings of D-Day?

19. In what ways do we see the leadership strengths of General Rommel providentially counteracted by the interference of his superior commanders?

20. How did the personal friendship between Winston Churchill and Franklin Roosevelt affect the cooperation of the Allies?

Bible Memory Verses

"So Joshua arose, and all the people of war, to go up against Ai: and Joshua chose out thirty thousand mighty men of valour, and sent them away by night." (Joshua 8:3)

"When I blow with a trumpet, I and all that are with me, then blow ye the trumpets also on every side of all the camp, and say, 'The sword of the LORD, and of Gideon.'" (Judges 7:18)

Episode 4

Deception, Intelligence, & Spying for D-Day

The English were the masters of military deception and spying. From the beginning of the war, their overall deception plan reflected Churchill's aphorism in its code name—"Operation Bodyguard." Episode 4 evaluates the use of spying in wartime and the specific operations of Allied forces to confuse the enemy. The plan created to protect England and eventually help bring about victory followed three general strategies: (1) deception—which, in relation to D-Day, included FUSAG—Patton's shadow command, and bogus radio communications indicating Calais as the D-Day target; (2) spies, double agents, fictitious sub-agents and other human assets in foreign high places as well as anti-Nazi underground cells in France and the Balkans; (3) and code and cipher intercepts that came from the captured Enigma ciphers, code named the "Ultra Secret."

1. What deceptions were used by King David in the escape and evasion phase of his life?

2. How did (General) Joshua, in the Bible book of that name, use spies to gather intelligence as he prepared to take the Promised Land?

3. In the Bible, what secret strategy did Gideon use in the defeat of the Midianites?

4. Who sent espionage agents to monitor the words of Jesus?

5. What happened to the Abwehr agents sent by Germany to England to gather secrets and transmit them back to German intelligence?

6. How did England acquire the Enigma ciphers?

7. How important was the Ultra Secret to the outcome of World War II?

8. Where were the decryption headquarters in England?

9. Why did the Germans believe General George Patton would lead the invasion?

10. What were some of the devices used to create the illusion of an army base in England?

11. How did the Germans react to attacks by the French underground resistance?

12. How were the decrypts used by the Allied armies in the theatres of battle?

13. Why was Calais a logical point of attack for D-Day?

14. How did Allied deception plans affect the German armored reserves in Western France?

15. Why did some underground resistance groups not work well together?

16. Did the British spy on the United States during the war?

17. What was the name of the American clandestine organization for spying and gathering intelligence?

18. Who was the American spy-master?

19. What did Winston Churchill believe about spying and deception?

20. Did the Allies use high-flying planes to photograph German positions?

Bible Memory Verses

"And Moses sent them to spy out the land of Canaan, and said unto them, 'Get you up this way southward, and go up into the mountain: And see the land, what it is; and the people that dwelleth therein, whether they be strong or weak, few or many; And what the land is that they dwell in, whether it be good or bad; and what cities they be that they dwell in, whether in tents, or in strong holds.'" (Numbers 13:17-19)

"And Saul pitched in the hill of Hachilah, which is before Jeshimon, by the way. But David abode in the wilderness, and he saw that Saul came after him into the wilderness. David therefore sent out spies, and understood that Saul was come in very deed." (I Samuel 26:3-4)

Episode 5
The Decision to Go

In Episode 5 we will examine in detail one of the most compelling elements of the D-Day story: the decision to go. The staggering complexities of organization, supply, training, manpower, weather, deception, and understanding the terrifying and confident enemy leadership and defenses had no single precedent in history from which to draw up a blueprint of attack. Upon the decision to launch this "mightiest endeavor" hung the future of millions and the direction of world history into the uncertain future. The Providences of God would shape the military, meteorological, and material landscape of that world-changing decision. The purposes of God would stand. From a providential and historical perspective, the decision to go takes place in the context of an amazing series of events within the camp of the enemy, including mistakes, decisions and indecisions, and confused reports, and the handicapping of Rommel's efforts by the high command. From this, we learn of both the power of the Lord to control weather and direct the course of human events, and the unique preparation of General Eisenhower for this one moment in time.

1. The original plan to invade France was planned for May, 1944. Why was it postponed?

2. Why was defeat of Germany in the Atlantic Ocean of paramount importance to the invasion?

3. Why did the Allies go to such extraordinary lengths to conceal their plans from the Germans?

4. What was General Eisenhower's command staff called?

5. What beach landing experiences did the Allied army in Europe have to draw on when planning the Normandy invasion?

____

____

____

____

6. Why were the coastal tidal charts so important to Eisenhower's planning?

____

____

____

____

7. The Army-Air Force and Navy insisted on what sort of weather for D-Day?

____

____

____

____

8. How many meteorology groups were consulted in the decision-making process?

____

____

____

____

9. Who briefed the generals about the weather reports?

10. When could the invasion have next been launched, if they had not gone on June 6?

11. What role did the Allied fighter planes and bombers play in the D-Day invasion?

12. How did General Rommel's superiors handicap his efforts to thwart the Allied invasion?

13. What important providential role did Adolph Hitler play that worked in favor for the Allies on D-Day?

14. How did the Allies solve the transportation problem to the beaches for D-Day?

15. What does "combined operations" mean?

16. What are ten items possibly carried by an airborne soldier?

17. What are glider troops?

18. What measures did the enemy take in the ocean and on the beaches to stop Allied vehicles?

19. What Scripture passages indicate that God controls the weather or the tides?

20. What are some biblical leadership qualities exhibited by General Eisenhower?

Bible Memory Verses

"Every purpose is established by counsel: and with good advice make war." (Proverbs 20:18)

"A man's heart deviseth his way: but the LORD directeth his steps." (Proverbs 16:9)

Episode 6

The Men of D-Day and Meaning of Manhood

Episode 6 turns our attention to the men of D-Day and to details of the Normandy invasion itself. We will discuss important lessons about manhood and courage as we look at the legacy of the U. S. Infantry on Utah Beach with the 4th Division, the 1st and 29th Divisions on Omaha Beach, and the 82nd & 101st Airborne Divisions which dropped inland of Utah Beach in the pre-dawn hours of the invasion. We will remember the story of the Bedford Boys, the Band of Brothers, and the stories of Teddy Roosevelt, Jr. and the Rangers of Pointe du Hoc. We will also hear poignant memories from veterans who journeyed back with us to the beaches of their youth on the 67th anniversary of the epic assault, men such as Donald Carter and Russell Pogue. Their stories, as well as many others, remind us of the great sacrifice that was made to liberate France and defeat the evil Nazi regime.

1. What U.S. divisions led the D-Day invasion of Normandy?

2. Why weren't the airborne troopers dropped in the right places?

3. What unusual providences favored the paratroopers on D-Day?

4. What obstacles had to be overcome by the infantry on the beaches?

5. Why didn't the Luftwaffe wreck the beach assaults from the air?

____

____

____

____

6. How did General Theodore Roosevelt, Jr. display biblical leadership qualities on Utah Beach?

____

____

____

____

7. What special skills did the Rangers display at Omaha Beach?

____

____

____

____

8. What tactical principles used by Lt. Richard Winters of the 101st Airborne at Brecourt Manor are still studied at military academies?

____

____

____

____

9. How did perseverance characterize the men of D-Day?

____

____

____

____

10. What are the effects of battlefield deaths on a community at home?

____

____

____

____

11 How did the men on the beaches react when there were few officers alive or capable of leading?

____

____

____

____

12. How should a soldier react when given a lawful order that will likely end in his own death?

____

____

____

____

13. What roles did the Navies play in the D-Day actions?

14. Is tactical aerial bombardment which unintentionally kills thousands of civilians (20,000 French in Normandy Campaign) unbiblical?

15. Should a commander always alert his troops about enemy reinforcements that just arrived at a position they are about to attack?

16. How did the invention of the Higgins Boat contribute to the defeat of Germany?

17. How did General Eisenhower hope to overcome the German advantages in tank quality and combat experienced troops?

18. Why did the Airborne troops have to capture the crossings of the Merderet River?

19. Once battle is engaged, are there any rules beyond self-preservation?

20. What role did the French underground play on D-Day?

Bible Memory Verses

"Be of good courage, and let us behave ourselves valiantly for our people, and for the cities of our God: and let the LORD do that which is good in his sight." (1 Chronicles 19:13)

"Through God we shall do valiantly: for he it is that shall tread down our enemies." (Psalms 60:12)

Episode 7
The Aftermath

Episode 7 offers a Christian perspective on the aftermath of D-Day. We will consider the cost of D-Day and its meaning, the Battle for Caen, the Falaise Pocket, and the Normandy Breakout. We will look at the Liberation of Paris, the Battle of the Bulge, and the ultimate surrender of the Nazi forces to the Allies, as well as England's misguided decision to vote out Winston Churchill from his post as Prime Minister as the war came to an end. Most importantly, we will answer these questions: What duties have we inherited from the men of D-Day; why must we remember D-Day and the men of D-Day; and what additional lessons can we learn as we look back nearly seventy years to this epic battle?

1. How did Hitler handicap his troops against "Operation Cobra?"

2. Why did the Normandy Campaign take so long to conclude?

3. What were the tragic results for the Allies in the attempted mass bombing of the German front lines in Operation Cobra?

4. What difficulties did Eisenhower have with the French Army in the drive toward Paris?

5. What happened to French collaborators after the fall of Paris to the Allies?

____

____

____

____

6. What American commander's army sliced through the German lines, cut off Brittany and made the encirclement of the German army possible?

____

____

____

____

7. What massive counter-attack did the German army make in December, 1944?

____

____

____

____

8. What two Allied Commanders-in-Chief were not in power when the Allies met at Potsdam to decide on the final disposition of World War II and its aftermath?

____

____

____

____

9. What does "Unconditional Surrender" mean?

10. How was post-war Germany divided among the Allies?

11. What were the Nuremburg Trials?

12. Why was the capture of Paris so important?

13. What are some common characteristics of World War II veterans we have interviewed?

14. What are some ways the world changed as a result of the Second World War?

15. What became of the key leaders of the war?

16. Why must we persevere after great victories such as D-Day?

17. On July 26, 1945 Prime Minister Winston Churchill was voted out of office—a mere two months following Germany's surrender to the Allies. What does this suggest about the perspective of the English citizens.

18. Are the losses and sacrifices of war, and especially D-Day, too painful to dredge up again and commemorate?

19. What good character traits can we learn from many of the men of D-Day?

20. What are some practical benefits of the Doctrine of Providence?

Bible Memory Verses

"Fret not thyself because of evildoers, neither be thou envious against the workers of iniquity. For they shall soon be cut down like the grass, and wither as the green herb." (Psalm 37:1-2)

"The LORD hath made known his salvation: his righteousness hath he openly shewed in the sight of the heathen." (Psalms 98:2)

Answer Key

Episode 1

1. Theology is literally the study of God. It includes His divine attributes, character, and works. A person's worldview reflects what he believes about God or about his own gods—everyone has a "theology."

2. Because a person's view of who God is and what He expects of him will inform his beliefs and behavior; a nation's cultural values will illustrate those theological commitments held by the shapers of that culture.

3. A Christian nation is one which historically regards the Bible as authoritative and professes an allegiance to Jesus Christ and God's ethical standards as enshrined in law. It means that, in its foundation, the laws and the covenants and the basic religious commitments of the nation are Christian, not necessarily that the current majority of the people are Christians.

4. Christendom refers to the parts of the world where Christianity has penetrated and become the dominant influence, shaping law structures, social mores, and cultural priorities of particular nations and peoples. It typically refers to the nations of Europe, including all the English speaking peoples, such as the United States, and their colonies, though it includes all nations that have claimed the Christian faith as the faith of their nation.

5. Churchill was raised in the Victorian Era in which English law and culture still showed reverence and respect toward its Christian heritage. Thus he was deeply affected by the values and mores of Christendom. Adolph Hitler rejected whatever remnants of Christianity he may have inherited in pre-war Austria and Germany and revered the ancient gods of the heathen ancestors, as well as his own reconstruction of a man-centered, evolutionary, fate-based worldview.

6. Churchill affirmed that the earth was the Lord's, and that liberty was upheld under a law order which recognized God as Sovereign; he affirmed the biblical notions of private property against statist confiscation; and he maintained that the rule of law, as established in such documents as the Magna Charta, was the standard. He affirmed the ancient order of Christendom.

7. Christian civilization.

8. Hitler admired aspects of the ancient Romans, especially their ability to conquer all their enemies, extend their empire through the use of military force, and erect symbols of conquest in their architecture.

9. The Roman Colosseum.

10. The Roman Eagle, the symbol of Jupiter used by the victorious armies, as well as victory wreaths. Hitler had plans to build a grand, Roman-style triumphal arch in Berlin to rival Paris' Arc de Triomphe, but this never materialized.

11. A. Evolutionism/Darwinian social theory
    B. Friedrich Nietzsche's philosophy of Übermensch
    C. The philosophy of Empire, as encapsulated in Rome

12. Richard Wagner

13. The Church should oppose and hold accountable civil magistrates who violate the Law of God. The Church should stand for truth, regardless of consequences.

14. The Ardeatine Caves Massacre. 335 Italian civilians were killed.

15. American journalist Sam Donaldson confronted Erich Priebke in the streets of Bariloche, Argentina, where Priebke had escaped after the war and lived for more than fifty years. Priebke openly admitted to Donaldson on camera of his involvement with the massacre and said he was simply "following orders". After the story aired on television, Priebke was arrested an extradited to Rome for trial.

16. Yes. There is no statute of limitations on murder.

17. Priebke was only held responsible for the murder of five of those killed during the massacre, and rather than being executed, he was placed under house arrest to live in Rome. This prompted a great outcry from many of the families whose relatives were killed during the massacre.

18. Winston Churchill

19. The Italian Campaign

20. The fall of Rome occurred on June 4, 1944, two days before Allied forces landed in Normandy on June 6.

Episode 2

1. National identity is related to the accumulation of cultural markers of a people through the centuries. At the heart of all cultural identities lie the basic presuppositions and the religious faith of the people. For instance, martial ardor and faith in the reason of autonomous man became the central tenants of French identity after 1790.

2. When a people's grip on their identity is loosened or broken, usually in the fires of adversity, they fall prey to the alien faith of a conqueror or suffer the oppression of a usurper from within their own ranks.

3. The withdrawal of biblical Christianity helped to smooth the way for France adopting humanistic philosophies of the seventeenth and eighteenth centuries. Another possible result of the destruction of the Huguenots of France and their subsequent mass emigration was the removal of the entrepreneurial and creative

propensities of the French. The Reformed Christians who were killed or left France tended to be the merchants, landowners, gentry, and artisans of the cities and towns of southern and western France.

4. The people of Northern Europe all stem from Germanic races of ancient lineage. The Franks and Normans and other tribes of ancient Gaul were cousins of their fierce northern neighbors. The modern descendents of those people have fought one another many times. Both Germany and France accepted a Darwinian, humanistic, evolutionary faith.

5. The Treaty of Versailles punished Germany for WWI. It included enormous, unpayable monetary reparations, loss of all colonies and some of its most profitable and important European territory, and humiliated them through loss of defensive and offensive military capability through restrictions on army and navy size and prohibition of building an air force. In 1918 the German people were starving, communist revolutions were erupting in various cities, and a generation of young men were in their graves after four years of war.

6. The French reduced their professional military forces dramatically after WWII and relied on their ability to call up the reserves in case of war. As German armies marched, and the Sudetenland, Austria, and Czechoslovakia fell under their sway in the late 1930s, France virtually ignored the buildup, issuing weak protests but not moving their soldiers to counter German moves. Eventually the French and British diplomatic policies would be termed appeasement—let Herr Hitler have his way in these small, historically German enclaves, and he will be satisfied and not harm us. When the attack on France came, they did not have the will or tactical expertise to slow or stop their defeat. In the end, they surrendered and submitted to a puppet regime known as the Vichy government.

7. Hitler wanted revenge for Germany's humiliation after WWI, and he wanted total hegemony over the European continent.

8. Phillipe Petain, who became the Marshal of France following distinguished military service during World War I, surrendered France to the Nazis in July of 1940 and became the leader of the France's new Vichy Regime, which answered to Nazi Germany.

9. To rounds up all Jews in France for deportation.

10. The Nazis exercised total control over France's foreign policy, occupied and controlled Paris, ordered the deportation of the Jews, and co-opted the French army.

11. Charles De Gaulle

12. World War II began on September 1, 1939, when Germany, without a declaration of war, invaded Poland.

13. "They that forsake the law praise the wicked: but such as keep the law contend with them." (Proverbs 28:4) "Thus saith the LORD, 'Execute ye judgment and righteousness, and deliver the spoiled out of the hand of the oppressor: and do no wrong, do no violence to the stranger, the fatherless, nor the widow, neither shed innocent blood in this place.'" (Jeremiah 22:3)

14. Winston Churchill was not fooled by Adolph Hitler's ruses and described Hitler's early moves as a "gathering storm" that he believed would be far more serious in scope for the people of Europe.

15. Proverbs 24:10 states: "If thou faint in the day of adversity, thy strength is small." Christian are to "endure hardness, as a good soldier of Jesus Christ" (2 Timothy 2:3) and not flinch when trials come. When faced with persecution, we are to persevere. In James 5:11, we read, "Behold, we count them happy which endure. Ye have heard of the patience of Job, and have seen the end of the Lord; that the Lord is very pitiful, and of tender mercy."

    Winston Churchill was an exemplar of this principle of perseverance during the Second World War. He encouraged the people of Great Britain to "never surrender" to the Nazi threat and to fight on through the dark days of early defeat. His inspiration shored up the English to endure and, with the Allies help, eventually defeat the Third Reich.

16. Prime Minister Neville Chamberlain. The Munich Agreement, which Chamberlain signed on September 30, 1938, which permitted Nazi Germany's annexation of the Sudetenland.

17. After the defeat of Britain and France, their armies were bottled up on the beaches of Dunkirk along the English Channel. The Germans paused to consider their options, and England sent an armada of every kind of ship that could float to rescue the soldiers, saving more than 300,000 soldiers from certain destruction by the victorious Germans.

18. The Battle of Britain, the largest air war waged to that point in history, proved to be critical for England, as the Royal Air Force beat back the Luftwaffe. The RAF's success against the Nazi air force held Hitler back from launching Operation Sea Lion, his planned amphibious invasion of the English coast.

19. God did oversee all the events of World War II. The Bible says he predestines all things to fulfill His purposes in history. Yet men are totally responsible for their behavior, so they will be held accountable for all the terrible tragedies and depraved actions committed in that conflict.

20. Believing the biblical doctrine of Providence gives us hope and confidence, knowing that God accomplishes His will for our good and His glory; our history and future are in His hands.

Episode 3

1. A leader must recognize he too is a man under authority, even if he is a king under the authority of God alone. General Dwight D. Eisenhower was under the authority of higher ranking generals, including the Joint Chiefs and the President of the United States. He had to learn obedience and respect as he demanded the same of his own inferiors. Some officers were deficient when it came to accountability and obedience and were defeated in battle or lost their positions for the failure to learn the lessons of submission.

2. A leader's self-confidence and superior abilities ought to be tempered by humility and a strong sense of duty. Understanding the chain of command and accepting accountability for one's actions help to secure confidence from superior officers and give a man advantages toward success or victory.

3. Ike delegated various aspects of a military operation to different experts, assembled the information, and gathered his staff to discuss the possibilities. He led the meetings and talked a great deal, but he accepted counsel and made his decisions based on consensus. He usually succeeded when his instructions were carried out.

4. The task before Eisenhower to liberate Europe was exceedingly complex. No single man could actually ask or answer all the necessary questions, much less create a workable plan. A team of counselors made the project possible, including British and Canadian leaders who would also play a significant role in the invasion.

5. To prepare for a military operation, a leader has many points to consider: (A) What are his human assets, both in terms of leadership for spearheading key objectives as well as adequate personnel in the field and air to get the job done? (B) What are his supplies—does he have the ships, planes, guns, ammunition, uniforms, food, etc. that he needs to carry out the mission? (C) What is the disposition and preparation of his enemy to defend against an attack, and what should be done to overcome these hurdles? (D) What sort of obstacles might he face in terms of terrain and weather related challenges? (E) What macro objectives do his superiors have that might impact his preparations, be they political or practical? (F) How does this operation fit in with the broader context of the war effort, and what should be done to prepare for what comes after?

6. Just as the Apostle Paul understood the philosophies and history of the Greeks and used that knowledge to witness concerning the Gospel to them, so too will a military leader be better able to predict what a given adversary may do in particular situations and thus move to counteract them in a strategically effective manner.

7. General Patton read General Rommel's pre-war book on armored tactics and studied the known details of his life. Armed with that knowledge as well as intelligence intercepts, he was able to counter Rommel's tactical moves in North Africa and contribute to Germany's defeat there.

8. FDR chose George C. Marshall to engineer the victory over the Axis from his position in Washington and trusted his judgment in the selection of key generals and admirals. He himself realized his great strength was communicating to the American people and thus left the military details to the experts. Hitler, on the other hand, made the macro decisions of military strategy without the actual training or competence to sustain victory over a prolonged conflict. His early victories reinforced his hubris, which providentially caused him to reinforce failure with bad decisions later on.

9. Hitler saw a thousand-year Reich dominating Europe, if not the world. The triumph of German culture, the destruction of the Jews and other perceived universal enemies, and the re-fashioning of history on the national socialist model were the stated and strongly pursued goals of the Nazi Party. Franklin Roosevelt viewed a world subordinated to an internationalist consortium called the United Nations, led by the United States and the other allied countries for the betterment of all mankind through the triumph of democracy. Winston Churchill looked to the future of a renewed British Empire ruling hand in hand with the other English speaking people, especially the United States, as liberty

and constitutionalism spread throughout the world to deserving nations. He looked for a resurrected Christendom, but was not opposed to a United Nations.

10. Nazi ideologues in the decades prior to the war developed a Darwinian, evolutionary-based belief in the innate superiority of the German "race." The resulting euthanasia practices of the 20s and 30s were easily transferred to mass executions and death camps in WWII. Untermenschen (sub-humans), including military POWs from Russia and Poland, were enslaved or killed outright.

11. When Patton disobeyed or violated rules, it reflected badly on his country and hurt his reputation, Ike had to discipline him. Conversely, when Bradley succeeded, Eisenhower gave him all the credit.

12. When a subordinate officer's strategic vision differs from his superior's, he should respectfully appeal. General Montgomery did not follow this approach, but acted arrogantly in pressing his perspective on General Eisenhower and the rest of the SHAEF staff.

13. Hitler took control of the German armored reinforcements prior to D-Day, yet he lived far from the theatre of conflict and was ignorant of the actual tactical and strategic situations of D-Day itself. Because his staff feared to wake him when the Allies attacked Normandy, the men and machines most capable of defeating the Allied beach assaults remained many miles from the scene of action.

14. Unlike flamboyant generals such as Patton and Montgomery, General Bradley was characterized by a humble attitude and trustworthiness; he regularly set aside his own ego for the greater mission and did not draw undue attention to himself.

15. National Socialism was indeed a real threat to Christendom as it sought to dethrone God and enshrine the "evolved" Aryan race as the ultimate ideal and to employ the power of the state to undermine liberty through tyrannical means.

16. Winston Churchill communicated a persevering spirit through his writings and most notably through his frequent radio messages to the people of Great Britain. Churchill's cry was "never surrender!"

17. The President delivered "fireside chats" over the radio to the American people. His powerful, persuasive, and confident voice brought hope and confidence of victory to millions of Americans whose sons and fathers were laying down their lives against the Axis Powers.

18. Research General Theodore Roosevelt, Jr., Captain Dick Winters, General Norman Cota, General James Gavin, General Matthew Ridgeway and their roles in the Normandy Invasion.

19. Rommel realized from past experience that once numerically superior Allied troops get ashore and inland, stopping them would be a monumental, perhaps impossible, task. He insisted the German forces defeat the Allies on the beaches. General Von Runsted and Hitler counteracted Rommel's requests, kept the reinforcements out of reach of the coast, and withheld the resources Rommel needed to succeed.

20. On the surface of things, their personal alliance may seem improbable. The relationship began with overtures by Churchill for sympathy and aid to fight Germany. Britain was standing alone under the onslaught of the terrible bombing campaign, but the United States was not ready for war, and an isolationist opposition to FDR made him reluctant to commit much to Britain's defense. Notwithstanding the political minefields, FDR did design ways and means to help Churchill and, in the end, joined him in a firm partnership to defeat Germany. The cooperation of the Allies was often strained, especially in their military relations, but the bond of affection between the leaders enabled the two nations to combine for victory in the end.

Episode 4

1. David used various subterfuges to survive. In one case, he was in the enemy's stronghold and was recognized as a killer of Philistines. He feigned madness and the enemy king released him as a crazy man. In another instance, he colluded with his wife Michal to place a dummy of himself in his bed to fool Saul's men, while she let David down through a window to escape.

2. Joshua sent two men to spy out the city of Jericho prior to the invasion of conquest that God had ordered Israel to conduct. They were spotted and hunted but were hidden by a woman named Rahab. The walls of the city fell down literally by God's hand, and the woman who hid the spies was saved alive by the conquerors.

3. Gideon's 300 men surrounded the host of enemy soldiers in the night, carrying torches covered by pottery jugs and trumpets that were typically used to signal

the attack on an enemy. At the appointed time, they smashed the pottery, revealing the torches and blew the horns, throwing the huge Midianite army into confusion. The Midianites slaughtered each other in the darkness from fear of having been surrounded by a mighty army which was descending upon them. God brought about a great victory through deception and subterfuge.

4. The Pharisees sent spies to record His words so they might trip Jesus up and condemn him. Jesus deflected their questions to avoid ensnarement.

5. They were all caught by MI-5 and Scotland Yard and were turned to act as double agents. Throughout the war, they sent misinformation back to the Abwehr, the German military intelligence, deceiving and lying so the Nazi decision-makers would have troops in the wrong places. The entire operation was known as "The double cross system" (XX), and it worked masterfully in deflecting the Germans from realizing the Allied intentions to land at Normandy.

6. In 1938 a Polish engineer memorized the Enigma coding machine components, was spirited out of Poland by British Intelligence, and reconstructed the machine, which encoded German infantry communications. Known as "the bronze goddess" and the "Ultra Secret" by the brilliant decrypt analysts, the Allies were able to know German military intentions throughout WWII. The reports helped the D-Day invaders know when and where the enemy were located, being able to identify 56 of the 58 German Divisions in France. They also acquired the Enigma coder for the German navy after the secret capture of a U-boat submarine, thus helping to win the Battle of the Atlantic and sinking most of the submarine fleet of Germany.

7. Those familiar with the value of the information gathered from decoded German intelligence through use of the Enigma machine noted that is was indispensable in defeating the Nazis. Winston Churchill told King George VI: "It was thanks to Ultra that we won the war." F. W. Winterbotham quoted General Eisenhower as saying that the Ultra was "decisive" in securing the Allies' victory.

8. Bletchley Park in the Town of Bletchley, Buckinghamshire, was an ancient site mentioned in the Domesday Book, now built up into a group of mixed architecture buildings. The British Government Code and Cipher School (GC&CS) was located there for the duration of the war.

9. The Germans believed he was the best Allied general and would not accept that he was suspended for slapping a soldier. Their assumptions were reinforced by the creation of the fictitious army that Patton was given command of, along

with made-up orders and misinformation concerning his missions that were broadcast in a way the Germans couldn't miss intercepting.

10. The Allies constructed inflatable tanks and airplanes, barracks for non-existent soldiers, and sent radio intercepts to non-existent officers and commands around the area. They allowed the German air force scouts to fly over and report back to their military intelligence about the build-up.

11. Attacks on German soldiers or installations were responded to in the harshest manner. If the perpetrators were captured, they would be tortured unmercifully and killed. If they weren't caught, sometimes reprisals were made on the civilian population. In a couple of cases, entire towns were massacred in revenge for underground resistance movement attacks.

12. Based on information about the dispositions of the enemy, the American fighter planes and bombers attacked concentrations of armor and troops in North Africa and Normandy. Furthermore, the commanding generals moved their combat formations to intercept troop movements based on intercepted and translated communiqués.

13. The historic city of Calais on the Normandy coast is the closest area to England. The white cliffs of Dover are about 21 miles away where there are beaches adequate for landing troops. The Allies tried to persuade the Germans that the attack would be launched against the Calais area. Thanks to the ingenious intelligence deception, five weeks after D-Day, German high command still thought the main attack was planned at Calais.

14. Hitler was so convinced the main Allied attack would land at Calais that he kept armored divisions near this area which could have counter-attacked at Normandy. Hitler still believed the D-Day attack was a feint, well after the move inland from the beaches of Normandy.

15. Many resistance cells operated independently of each other and, in France, many of the underground groups were communists and were either run directly from Moscow or were otherwise hostile to non-communist resisters.

16. British intelligence services operated in every Allied and Axis country.

17. The Office of Strategic Services (OSS), which became the Central Intelligence Agency (CIA) after the war.

18. A highly decorated WWI veteran (including Medal of Honor) and attorney from western New York, "Wild Bill" Donovan ran the American intelligence and counter-intelligence forces in WWII. He had a close personal relationship with FDR but was disliked by Douglas MacArthur and J. Edgar Hoover. Donovan supervised sabotage and spying operations in many places.

19. He loved deceiving the enemy and studied all the intelligence reports every day, using the information for strategic decision-making.

20. The British developed high-altitude photography (30,000 feet) after they invented a way to blow warm air over the lenses of the cameras, which otherwise fogged at 8,000 feet altitude.

Episode 5

1. The Allies determined that the planning and preparation were still inadequate. They increased the number of invasion beaches from two to five and increased the number of men for the first waves. More supplies were needed, along with more ships, as well as increased disinformation to fool the enemy about their plans.

2. Millions of soldiers and thousands of tons of supplies had to be transported to England from the United States. With German U-Boats sinking merchant and military vessels, the defeat of the German navy in the North Atlantic took on vital importance for D-Day. The Ultra secret and valorous sailors made that possible.

3. Because there were only two feasible places to land on the French coast—Calais and Normandy—those areas could be especially fortified to resist attack. By convincing the Germans that the assault would come at the other site, or at least creating enough confusion that the Germans divided their forces, the concealment of plans increased the possibility of success.

4. Supreme Headquarters Allied Expeditionary Forces (SHAEF)

5. The British/Canadians executed a raid on the French coastal city of Dieppe in August of 1942. While gaining experience in combined operations, the Allies took 60% casualties, lost 96 aircraft, and were forced to withdraw. They did discover, however, that beach landings could be done and what elements would be most important for future landings. That experience was used for

more successful landings in North Africa, Sicily, and Italy, all the information of which was used to plan for D-Day.

6. More than 6,000 Allied ships would eventually be used for the invasion. The tidal depths, times, and power would have to align in order for the landing craft, tanks, and troops to get ashore.

7. Airborne did not want any ground fog or mist and needed clear visibility to find drop zones at night. The Navy needed smooth seas and low tides. The odds that good enough weather would occur in June were about 30-1.

8. At least four different groups of weathermen were consulted, the Admiralty, Air Forces, U.S. and UK weather services; they used different methods of prognostication and their predictions were often contradictory.

9. The Chief Meteorologist of General Eisenhower's staff, 28-year-old Group Captain J.M. Stagg, a "dour but canny Scot."

10. June was twice as good as May and four times as good as July. Only one day in July was propitious; the next potential date would have been in August, providing the Germans with better than two more months of preparation.

11. A *sine qua non* of the invasion was total Allied air superiority. This was achieved in the days and months leading up to the invasion. On the day before D-Day and after, the Allied bombers plastered targets in many places along the French coast. On D-Day itself, Allied fighters and bombers flew round-the-clock missions and virtually kept the Luftwaffe out of the skies.

12. General Rommel's superiors did not allow him to command all the resources to counteract the invasion. Only Hitler himself could release the armored reinforcements. Rommel was denied the man-power to effectively defend the Atlantic Wall.

13. The Fuehrer not only retained the sole power to release the Panzer divisions reinforcements, he slept late on June 6th, having given orders not to be disturbed. When the HQ generals like Jodl got the news of the invasion, they were afraid to awaken him. While he slept, the vanguard of three million soldiers stormed ashore at Normandy.

14. Many different ships were slated to transport troops and equipment but the "Landing Ship, Tank" (LSTs) and the Higgins boats (LCVP) ferried the men and machines to the beach. Special floating tanks did not do so well, foundering in the waves.

15. The combination of army or marine infantry and naval forces working together to land on beaches from the sea.

16. There are many possible items carried by airborne troops: ammunition, weapons—knives, rifles, sub-machine gun—mortar tube, mortar base, machine gun, grenades, matches, New Testament, musette bag, medical supplies, socks, cigarettes, chocolate, sewing kit, rope, C-rations, chewing gum, cricket, shovel, flashlight, watch, playing cards, mess kit, blanket, gas mask, etc.

17. Special airborne troops who went into battle from plywood and fabric planes towed by bombers and cut loose to glide into the fields of Normandy. They could carry infantry or heavy weapons and jeeps for the paratroopers.

18. The Germans laid millions of mines, built iron bowties into the surf to rip up boats, and planted various other obstacles to stop the cross-channel invaders.

19. Job 28:25-30; 12:15; 37:10 Psalm 33:7; 147:15-18, etc.

20. He sought the counsel of men on his staff (in many counselors there is wisdom); He accepted accountability for his actions; he was able to persevere during severe trials.

Episode 6

1. 1st, 29th, 4th Infantry; 82nd and 101st Airborne

2. Several factors confused the airborne drops on D-Day: overcast skies, fearful pilots, German anti-aircraft fire, and a general failure to properly identify drop zones.

3. The German defenders of Normandy were taken by surprise, key German commanders were not with their troops, and haphazard and scattered drops prevented the enemy from identifying the airborne troops' strategies and

targets. Lack of communication between German Generals and Hitler and armored forces that were too far behind the beaches also kept the Germans from launching an effective counter-attack.

4. Besides rifle, machine-gun and artillery fire by the Germans, the infantry had to get past minefields, anti-tank traps, hundreds of yards of open beach, and defenders in concrete bunkers and entrenchments.

5. The German Air Force was effectively neutralized by American bombers and fighters. Many were shot down or destroyed on the ground. The Allied air attack completely controlled the skies.

6. He did not worry about his own life in the face of duty and danger. His concern for those under him was to set the example for them that would reinforce their courage and resolve to do their duty.

7. The Rangers fired grappling hooks and ropes up the cliffs of Pointe du Hoc and climbed the cliffs to drive off the defenders who had deadly targeting of the beaches.

8. Lt. Winters demonstrated the ability to lead a small unit attack and adapt to the realities of a previously unknown situation. He and his men of Easy Company knocked out a German battery and its defenders through the use of surprise and aggressive coordinated small unit tactics.

9. After suffering heavy casualties at Omaha Beach and in various fire-fights behind the beaches, the American troops persisted in following their leaders to capture the enemy positions. They overcame every obstacle and kept advancing until the enemy was driven back and off the beaches.

10. The usual immediate effects on communities in WWII were grief and renewed resolve to defeat the enemy. In the case of Bedford, Virginia, the percentage of men killed, mostly on D-Day , effected the community for generations since so many of the families were either related to the soldiers or knew them well.

11. Men of lower rank stepped forward and filled the gaps of leadership.

12. The soldier has taken an oath to do that very act if called upon. “No greater love hath any man than to lay down his life for his friend.”

13. The navies of the United States and the United Kingdom carried the troops to the beaches, fired their large guns into the enemy positions, and provided reinforcements and hospital ships to the battle. Without the naval competence and unwavering efforts on their part, the assault could not have begun, been sustained, or succeeded.

14. This is a very controversial issue because military targets were often near civilian areas. Unwilling noncombatants also worked in the factories and on the trains being attacked. Legitimate military targets can be attacked from the air, but precision bombing should avoid non-military casualties. Terror bombing to kill civilians out of hand is immoral.

15. General Eisenhower was faced with this very decision. Since the knowledge of the new troop positions would not change the attack in any way and might negatively affect the morale of the attackers, he chose not to inform his Division Commanders.

16. This boat, designed by Andrew Jackson Higgins, enabled the infantry to get to the beaches in relative safety, then exit onto the beaches over the front ramp, without having to climb over the sides. It is hard to see how the success of the beach attacks could have been effected without the Higgins Boats.

17. Ike hoped to overwhelm the enemy with numerical superiority in troops, armor, and supplies. ("Quantity has a quality all its own.") Furthermore, his air forces would drive the enemy from the skies and destroy the German armor, troops, and supplies on the ground.

18. The capture of Sainte-Mère Église cut off the roads to the beaches. The Germans had to recapture the town to contain the beach landings. The counter-attacks would have to cross the Merderet River. The Airborne soldiers had to seize bridges and causeways in order to stop the German counter-attacks.

19. Once battle is engaged, your own self-preservation is subordinated to duty within the confines of known biblical precept.

20. The Maquis and other French underground forces attacked military and communications targets and bridges. Eisenhower claimed their contribution to the success of D-Day was significant.

Episode 7

1. The Fuhrer ordered his field armies to hold every position and fight to the last man, thus handicapping them from strategic retreats or avoiding Allied traps. In the end, they were almost surrounded and lost more than half their forces in the Falaise Pocket. Also, Hitler's retribution for the attempt on his life included the deaths of dozens of generals and colonels, some of them at the highest levels of command, like Generals Rommel and Von Kluge.

2. The roads to Paris passed through hedgerows through the French countryside, virtually impenetrable by men or machines. Although outnumbered, the Germans defended well the villages and towns and the fields between the hedges.

3. They accidently bombed their own front lines also, causing hundreds of deaths including Major General Leslie McNair.

4. The French generals wanted to subordinate the overall Allied efforts in trapping and defeating the Germans to the capture of Paris by the French army.

5. Some were executed; others were shaved and shamed through the streets.

6. General George Patton and the U.S. Third Army

7. The Ardennes Offensive, known to the Allies as "The Battle of the Bulge."

8. Franklin Roosevelt died in April, 1944 and Winston Churchill was turned out of office by the voters in July, 1944.

9. It is the traditional demand made by American commanders to a defeated foe begun by Ulysses S. Grant in the War for Southern Independence. It means the leaders of the losing side must surrender without any conditions—placinge themselves and their country totally at the disposal and mercy of the conqueror. This controversial policy was used against both Germany and Japan.

10. The country was divided into two separate nations, East and West Germany. The Russians controlled the Eastern portion, the United States, England, and France controlled the Western part. The city of Berlin was also divided into four parts among the conquerors within the East German zone.

11. They were the post-war trials of high-ranking Nazi officials and officers for "crimes against humanity." Ironically, the Russians had committed many atrocities also but were, nonetheless, part of the tribunal by virtue of their key role among the victorious allies.

12. Though not a militarily strategic city, Paris symbolized the history and soul of the French people, and taking it away from the Germans after a four-year occupation signaled the freeing of France and the eventual destruction of the Third Reich.

13. They are humble, realizing God's grace in preserving them through the war. They remember their comrades killed in battle as the real heroes. They all say that they were just doing their duty.

14. International boundaries changed dramatically as Germany and Japan lost all of their conquered territory and much of their own prewar land. A "Cold War" ensued for the next forty-five or so years between the free nations of the West and the enslaved nations under the U.S.S.R.

15. General Eisenhower became President of the United States for two terms and leader of the free world. He lived on, much beloved, till 1969, dying at the age of 79. After a few years of political exile, Winston Churchill was reelected as Prime Minister. He lived to the age of 91, a hero and "man of the century" to many. Hitler died in his bunker in Berlin just before the final overwhelming of the Reich by the Allies. Stalin increased his oppression of the Russian people and the newly enslaved nations he conquered in the war. He died in 1953, and his empire crashed in 1990. General Bradley became the Chairman of the Joint Chiefs of Staff, served as an advisor during the Vietnam War. His memoir/autobiography was well-regarded by historians. His last public appearance was in celebration of the election of Ronald Reagan in 1981. He died at the age of 88, the last five-star General of the United States. General Patton died from injuries received in a car accident in Germany shortly after the war ended. General Montgomery remained a man of modest means and was raised to Viscount then Earl. He held the position of Chief of the Imperial General Staff. He remained critical of Ike and other fellow generals of the war, controversial to the last, dying at the age of 88. Lt. Richard Winters, promoted several more times in WWII, retired from the army after the war and lived a peaceful and modest life until 2011. His grave in Ephrata, Pennsylvania simply reads Richard Winters, World War II, 101st Airborne.

16. The fight must go on till the enemy is totally defeated. If we rest on our laurels prematurely, the enemy will always counterattack and drive us to defeat.

17. The English citizenry was incredibly short-sighted to vote out the man from office who had courageously guided them through one of the defining crises in the history of Great Britain. Their actions also smacked of ingratitude and a lack of appreciation for all that Churchill did on their behalf to confront and ultimately defeat Nazi Germany.

18. God commands us to remember all His mighty acts, to know of our fathers' pasts, and to seek their wise counsel. Commemoration and remembrance are excellent and useful way to accomplish those goals. Honoring our fathers for their willingness to preserve our liberty helps us pursue the same goal for our own children.

19. Courage, Sacrifice, Loyalty, Perseverance, Duty.

20. It gives us hope and confidence that God controls the past, present, and future and that history is following, without fail, the path that He has ordained.

Select Bibliography for Further Reading

Episode 1

Death in Rome: The Ardeatine Caves Massacre in WWII, by Robert Katz, MacMillan Company, 1967

By What Standard, by Dr. R.J. Rushdoony, Ross House Books, 1958

Hitler's Pope: The Secret History of Pius XII, by John Cornwell, Viking, 1999

The History of Christianity and Western Civilization Study Guide, by Joshua Phillips, Vision Forum, 2010

Adolph Hitler, by John Toland (2 vols.), Doubleday & Company, 1976

Churchill: A Biography, by Roy Jenkins, Hill and Wang, 2001

Churchill and War, by Geoffrey Best, Hamilton & London, 2005

The Day of Battle: The War in Sicily and Italy, 1943-1944, by Rick Atkinson, Henry

Holt and Company, 2007

Monte Cassino, by David Hapgood and David Richardson, Da Capo Press, 2002

Episode 2

Churchill: A Biography, by Roy Jenkins, Hill and Wang, 2001

Churchill and War, by Geoffrey Best, Hamilton & London, 2005

Adolph Hitler, by John Toland (2 vols.), Doubleday & Company, 1976

The Miracle of Dunkirk, by Walter Lord, Viking Press, 1982

With Wings Like Eagles: The Battle of Britain, by Michael Korda, Harper, 2009

Episode 3

Adolph Hitler, by John Toland (2 vols.), Doubleday & Company, 1976

Churchill: A Biography, by Roy Jenkins, Hill and Wang, 2001

Churchill and War, by Geoffrey Best, Hamilton & London, 2005

Franklin and Winston: An Intimate Portrait of an Epic Friendship, by Jon Meachum, Random House, 2003

Knight's Cross: A Life of Field Marshall Rommel, by David Fraser, Harper Collins, 1993

Patton: A Genius for War, by Carlos D'Este, Harper Collins, 1995

A Soldier's Story, by Omar Bradley, Holt, 1951

Monty, by Nigel Hamilton (2 vols.), McGraw Hill, 1981

Eisenhower: A Soldier's Story, by Carlos D'Este, Holt, 2002

Episode 4

The Ultra Secret: How the British Broke the German Code, by F. W. Winterbotham, Orion Paperbacks, 2000

Ike's Spies: Eisenhower and the Espionage Establishment, by Stephen Ambrose, University Press of Mississippi, 1999

The Secret War: The Inside Story of the Code Makers and Codebreakers of World War II, by Mike Paterson, David & Charles PLC, 2007

Maquis: The French Resistance at War, by George Reid Millar Cassell, 2003

Living and Fighting with the French Underground, by David Swanzy, UniqPublishing/UniqWare, 2011

The Man Who Never Was (FILM), by Ewen Montagu (1953)

Episode 5

The Great Crusade, by Dwight D. Eisenhower, Johns Hopkins University Press, 1997

Forecast for Overlord: General Eisenhower's Chief Weatherman Tells the Story Behind the Decision to Launch the Normandy Invasion, by J.M. Stagg, Ian Allan, 1971

Eisenhower: A Soldier's Story, by Carlos D'Este, Holt, 2002

Eisenhower at War, 1943-1945, by David Eisenhower, Collins, 1986

D-Day, June 6, 1944: The Climactic Battle of World War II, Stephen E. Ambrose, Simon & Schuster, 1994

Episode 6

D-Day, June 6, 1944: The Climactic Battle of World War II, by Stephen E. Ambrose Simon & Schuster, 1994

Decision in Normandy, by Carlos D'Este, Dutton, 1983

June 6, 1944: The Voices of D-Day, by Gerald Astor, St. Martin's Press, 1994

D-Day: The First 72 Hours, by William F. Buckingham, Tempus, 2004

The D-Day Atlas: The Definitive Account of the Allied Invasion of Normandy, by John Man, Facts on File, 1994

Band of Brothers: From Normandy to Hitler's Eagle Nest, by Stephen E. Ambrose, Simon & Schuster, 1992

Currahee! A Paratrooper's Account of the Normandy Invasion, by Donald R. Burgett, HMCO, 1967

Theodore Roosevelt Jr.: The Life of a War Hero, by Paul H. Jeffers, Presidio, 2002

The Bedford Boys: One American Town's Ultimate Sacrifice, by Alex Kershaw, Da Capo, 2003.

If Chaos Reigns: The Near Disaster and Ultimate Triumph of the Allied Airborne Forces on D-Day, by Flint Whitlock, Casemate, 2011

Osprey Books

Osprey Publishing of Great Britain publishes a multitude of modestly priced books on many aspects of military history. Their World War II collection is extensive and brilliantly written and illustrated. Of their WWII selection, the following are highly recommended for studying America's involvement in the Normandy Invasion.

Overlord: The D-Day Landings, by Ken Ford and Steven Zaloga

The D-Day Companion, by 12 World-leading Historians

D-Day 1944 (1): Omaha Beach, by Steven Zaloga and Howard Gerrard

D-Day 1944 (2): Utah Beach, by Steven Zaloga and Howard Gerrard

Rangers Lead the Way: Pointe Du-Hoc, D-Day, 1944, by Steven Zaloga and Howard Gerrard

Episode 7

The Invasion of France and Germany, 1944-1945, by Samuel Eliot Morison, Little Brown, 1957

The Mighty Endeavor: The American War in Europe, by Charles MacDonald, Da Capo Press, 1992

A Time for Trumpets: The Battle of the Bulge, by Charles B. MacDonald, Harper Perennial, 1997

A Soldier's Story, by Omar Bradley, Holt, 1951

Eisenhower: A Soldier's Story, by Carlo D'Este, Holt, 2002

Patton: A Genius for War, by Carlo D'Este, Harper Collins, 1995

Monty, by Nigel Hamilton (2 vols.), McGraw Hill, 1981